BOHEMIAN BRIDE

Heart of Glory Publishing

www.ballardjanae.com

ISBN: 978-1-7350082-0-2

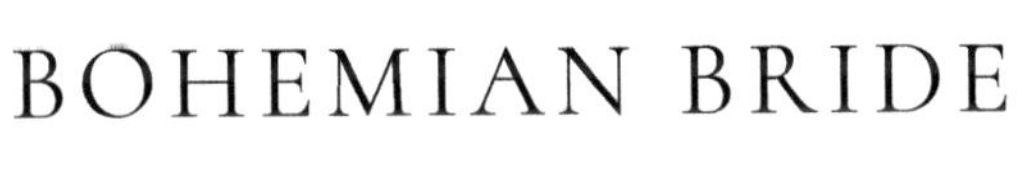
BOHEMIAN BRIDE

BOHEMIAN BRIDE

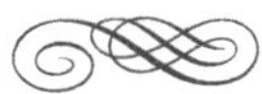

PROSE + POETRY

JANAE BALLARD

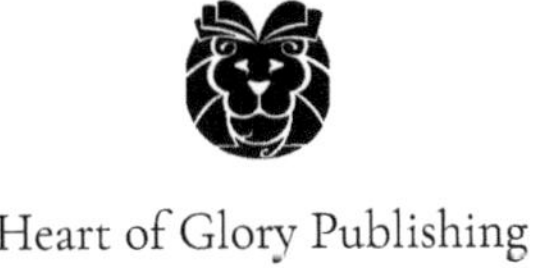

Heart of Glory Publishing

DEVOTION

Do not waste a moment of devotion!
Commit to God your hand, and He will hold you.
Love your work, but work *from* Love...
Do not waste a moment of devotion!
Commit to God your heart, and He will mold you—
To use your gifts how no one else can;
Inspiring special souls in eternal purpose.
Do not waste a moment of devotion!
Commit to God your all, and you will behold Him—
Taken places eyes haven't seen, nor ear heard.
Never trade the Creator for creation.

I

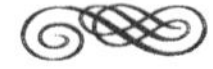

LOVE BASIS

LOVE FORMULA

Whoever desires true love
Must always love sincere—
Love kindly, love selfless,
Love unconditional.

For, isn't this love lasting?
And isn't this love real?
Thus it cannot begin unless
You are first a lover!

WHERE LOVE IS BORN

Why long for love as if you know it?
To know it is to have it for yourself.
You chase feelings that you think bring
Happiness, but this is felt when you rest.

LOVE CHASES

Are you searching for love?
Know it takes many forms and shapes:
A friend, a child, a spouse,
In heart, in faith, in grace.
Nothing true is sought without being found.
If love were near, you'd have it;
Like the sudden wind, it comes or is absent.
The Spirit of love blows unexpectedly.
It finds you first; it chases.
What will you do when it comes?
Will you give reverence?
Will you take it for granted?
No good's withheld from a good soul.
Either you're not a lover, or
They're not ready to be known, and
More salutary loves are for discovery now.
Or maybe you're too great a lover
To be ruined by this world—warm and moved
By hopeful intrigue and intuition
Like a whispering air in someone's ear.
What your heart calls will hear.

LOVE ETIQUETTE

Love delicate.
Hold what you love so gently
That you can let go if needed.
Don't crush it trying to control it;
Love is sweet but far too bold.
You won't ever get around it.
You'll never understand
The magnitude it can reach—
How deep it can be,
How high it can make you feel...
Don't force yourself into those heights
Lest you fall.
Embrace it softly.
Love delicately.

MERE INFATUATION

A thousand eyes
Of infatuation
Are incomparable
With the worth of two
That see pass hurt
And see to loving you.

LOVE WELL

Pulled away from water,
Made to sit in salt—
Growing calloused
And resentful;
Heartache for love lost,
Or perhaps it never was,
Or one day will be—
But love doesn't hurt you;
It is in harmony with life,
Both refining and refreshing.
It holds balance within;
No separation or disconnect.
It will not sap you but is full
Of giving and filling
With everything you need
To feel and know that
All is well.

SOUL VALUE

Who knows your worth when it's hidden by shame?
Who sees you when you don't stand out?
Who remembers you despite potential?
Who seeks your best while you're self-destructing?
Who would, soul-to-soul, remain?

STEP OF FAITH

Just because love is present
Doesn't mean I won't be anxious; besides...
Wouldn't the realest things in life
Feel groundbreaking to approach?
What love does mean, though,
Is I'll take the step.

LIMITLESS LOVE

Love has made
A ship to sail,
Through the heavens,
God to man.
Limitless!
It builds a bridge.
Love has made
Technology
So you would be
A call away,
But is love restrained
If this were not?
Would you not be
Merely
A letter away?
A sea away?
A desire away?

2

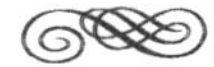

WANDERING

UNIVERSAL ARTISAN

It's a yearly routine for me to go to the festival.
Am I going to see you when it enters town?
I am planning to wear my red shirt, lined in red frills.
It'll be here for the weekend. Can't wait to meet you there!
I will be the red thread
Spinning, spinning, spinning
Amid artisan's air.
Weaving crowds the way they spread themselves into their fashions.
See if you can spot me—magically disappearing—see if you can stop me.
I think I'll be starving by the time we speak; if you are too,
We could grab a bite to eat! My treat! And you can share more about
Your work, your ventures, your beliefs—your
continued faithfulness,
No matter cultural surroundings. Also, their qualities and the beauties you witness.
I'd love an update on all that's changed,
Especially the people, their stories, their lives—piece in piece with yours.

A FAITHFUL CALL TO BELIEVE

Faith does wonders;

Whether the Christian faith
Or not, it's a confidence and hope,
And both do wonders.

It does not waste its life in fear
Nor worry over judgment.
It does not waste time complaining,
But will boldly state want and go expectant.

A journey of faith opens eyes to what we care about,
Providing passion against the deal of darkness,
Keeping you striving for your deal of peace.

Full of capability
And high capacity,
It lives reaching until
That final sunken day.

And its persistence,
Wanting to go further,

Can break boundaries again!

Faith, if placed in an object—
In a Savior, a faithful, sparing friend
Who can take over, continues
To encourage upheld eyes.

God has always honored faith
And will so, through Christ,
For the afterlife.

FOUR GIRLS WHO LIVED A THOUSAND LIVES

Would you believe a story of four girls who lived a thousand lives?
Their primes full of laughter, great adventure, and concerns—
Horrified, almost helpless at the ill-fated world.

They would expand time by traveling paper lines, bridging into
New walks of life, and discovering infinite possibilities.
Suited in panoply obtaining wisdom like a fitted helmet.

They'd invite you to read into their journeys of living, dying, and
Living another. The cleverness of rebirth relying on the select novelist's
Transcendence—their faith, preservation, fleeing death's sorrowful grip.

Lighthearted girls who would know bitter ends if not for stumbling across
Staircases to heaven's righteous lands. If they were not less than
Four snowflakes on the mountainside drifting alongside

Soldiers fallen in heaps of brutal cries, frozen, silenced by the blizzard.

And through forest finding humanity in cubs trailing a bear's fatherhood.

Drifting alongside windows spotting two tiny girls, two little boys,

Four innocent siblings running wooden cottage floors, ringing bells in Nativity joy.

A thousand lives lived in a thousand faces, places upon places, originating

From a book club where they'd bury their alienation and sojourn together into graces ahead.

TRAIL BLAZE

Revive the dreams of your past!
Don't allow them to slip away into
Satan's hands and thieving games.

Find the fragments of hope
Once had in your inner child,
Now scattered like barrettes,

Buttons, marbles, and lost cards.
Gather them!
They are not destroyed!

Though seemingly gone for good,
Especially with you no longer wanting
Anything, nothing so hard and hurtful

To go after, love to cherish! Love love
More than sadness, more than
The hatred that comes after it passes.

Then you won't have to fight for what you had;
It will blaze again from inside you to hell's shame.
All returning incredibly reclaimed.

SECRET GARDENS

Do you remember the movies that told of love and gardens—scenes of a woman in a creamy dress dusting through chocolate soil among countless flowers as lovely as but no more than her? And how a fellow always seemed to look over gently, from a balcony paid no mind. At that moment, he'd seen the softest radiance and gain a passion of the most innocent and faithful kind.

I visit the botanical gardens so often since the veil's been lifted from my eyes. How many times before such sights were missed or taken for granted? Now I adore creation, and if only I, I will behold it all alone. Yet I too feel, but not of man's inspection, quiet protection gazing from above, ever so sweetly, holding purest affections I paid no mind for a lifetime before.

ON THE TRAIL OF LOVE

You and I were on the trail of love
Until something made you hesitate,
And I had to walk alone.
Love told me to let you go,
And how it was right to carry on.
You hated me for it,
But the ends were prosperous
Because you were stuck by fear,
And I dared to follow hope.
I knew there could be better
And was led further into love—
Love that makes you wiser,
More confident, and sure.
Love which grants peace
And all we ever long for.
By this, our faith has greatened,
Having a clearer direction.
We may not cross paths again,
But both know what lies ahead
Is a favorable destination.

AMASS

Amass your flowers, child.

Who should weed out your wild?

Dance in the dusk,

Kiss the moonlight,

Wander and cry

By the truth you find.

Feel your burning heart,

Give homage to the artist,

Wear your graceful flowers

Clothed daisy, lily, rose.

Amass and sow

Seeds of harmony.

Sing, sing the rebuttal of woe.

Chime into the sights you go.

Life-giving, life giving.

Tell the city. Tell the world.

BUILDING BRIDGES

We took the plank
From our eyes
And built a bridge
For the lost
To find their way
To a place of love
And outspread arms
Where we're a
Body of friends
Of excellent reason
For being understanding.

BLESSINGS

Encountering
A winter warmth,
A songful stream,
A critter's subtle
Winsomeness, or
A person who is
Fresh air,
Music to ears,
Butterflies in my gut,
And light in my eyes
All at once
Are universal charms
I am too grateful for
To call luck.

MAN OVER THE MOON

Some pray to the moon,
Some inquire of it.
Some wait on the moon,
Some stay for it.
Some create beneath the moon,
Some write about it.
Someone wanted the moon
To be a part of life's story.

NO IMITATION

We hold a story no one else can tell.
I told you about the forest.
You told me about the ocean.
I am soil. You are sand.
I bear marks of foxes.
You bear marks of Grapsidae crab.
I've experienced scarring of stones,
Splitters of wood, and pitfalls in the mire.
You've experienced the scorching sun,
Rashes of grain, and slips into suffocating waters.
I've encountered the boar. I understand the fawn.
You've encountered the eel and understand the otter.
We learn from each other.
We meet together but live by different roots.
I am the center of my plane.
You are the corner of your domain.
My sisters spread throughout the north-east.
Your brothers spread throughout the south-west.
And they talk about innumerable, exclusive exposures.
We hold observations no one else can see.

HUMAN COMPASS

You don't have to carry a backpack on your shoulder or
travel the globe.
You wear your heart on your sleeve, and leave
impressions everywhere you go.
Your life encounters step by step make a difference.
Life is a grand adventure, no matter where you stand.
The moment you are born is your arrival;
Navigate, celebrate, and triumph—
The opportunity where love shows how it lingers at
departure.
You have been known from your hair to your feet.
Some have visited your eyes and recall them fondly.
Your lips for someone are a memory of painful words
or pleasantries.
How you walk is a compass that another could follow.
You are a world map, and so are others.
What has been your experience when you've met them?
Did you see something spectacular, did you learn
something?
Did they tell you their history, were they anything
like you;
Or a brand new discovery your being needed to know?

CURIOUS, LOST, AND ASSURED

Curious people
Molding out new creations.

Lost people
Searching out new pleasures.

Assured people
Soaking in old favors
That occurs throughout all existence.

BLUSH

Fluster and squirm, don't know why.
I'm used to trapping butterflies;
Let them go in wedding ties,
Lies.

The kindness killer came in silence;
Taunted beauty to keep in private,
Radiating too much, not right...
Why?

Kiss your father, hug your friends,
Dimming care is oppressive darkness.
Believe that love soars and spreads,
Natural.

FLOATING AWAY

Am I drowning in a bottle of shaken water, or am I free?

Free to learn to swim. To combat the waves. Find victory.

Is there a voice holding me under? Is it them or me?

Am I bound to their surrender, or can I rise above the sea?

Will I enslave chains? Can I break those around my feet?

Perhaps I am hopeless; perhaps I am already floating away.

GOOD LIFE

Hours redeemed
By wise guys,
No regrets
In the good life.

THE SEA SOUL SPEAKER

When the beach is quiet, the air is different,
The tide is speaking,
Prettiest sweet nothings rolling off its tongue,
Sharing secrets in the night.
And I've found the tellings have glimmers of life.
What it knows, it knows in depth
From the deepest blue to brightest reflections.
Listen at the late hour to its whisper.
A voice wades clear in the soul: the eye that sees,
The ear that hears beyond.
What precious moments, and you a witness! To such
Vastness or nothingness...

LET THERE BE LIGHTS TONIGHT!

Come decorate the night in fireworks with me!
I want to celebrate the light we see—
The spark,
The fire,
And how it all began.

SOUL POCKET

Carry someone everywhere you go,
A voice to recognize that you belong—
The sound of steadfast love and inspiration,
A soul that knows by life the path you're taking.

3

LOST HEART

BLIND VISITOR

When you came, how did you enter?
Haphazardly? Or through the door?
To stop strangers in their tracks,
I left my heart on the welcome mat;
My values, my interest, written in red.
How long would you wait for me?
Would you do so patiently, or would you go?
I left warning signs were they read?
When you came, was it for me?
If so, how can you leave?

A POT OF LOVE AND ASH

I was turning into ashes
Crossing fires, loving Death—
A vessel pouring water from a mortal heart.

With so much pain, you'd presume I knew it wrong,
But whether or not it was the way didn't dawn.

Not until a potter said, "give it hatred,"
Did I look up, recovered by His tears...

The matter needed life, not sacrifice alone.
Mortal death can save nothing.
It could only keep my love from living.

A HOPEFUL INNOCENCE

My hope was innocence, so it left once I misthought
My sin was evidence it was gone.
Still, I was perfect for someone, for whom beauty
Was innocence—
A classic radiance I knew was formed from faith.
But I lost all these things
When they left for hopes to find one more "beautiful,"
A greater glow.
I should have taken this at face value, but I did not;
I was tainted,
And all my hope was innocence, prior to
The object of
My faith's return, with the reminder that my innocence
Is always my hope in Him.

LOVE SICKNESS

You rest in my mind like the sea rest
And then sometimes as restless,
Gently swaying or as raging waves.
You rest in my mind like the sea rest,

And I lay on the sea as in God's hands,
Dependent on His stillness; closed eyes by fear,
And I am seasick, but open wonder brings
Praise and trust in the moment.

I gain from the wind and the ride
Balance, strength, and new sight when
God rests in my mind despite shipwreck, I'm
Blessed by the birds and sun gleaming overhead.

MY HEART SAYS LOVE IS RED

If love is red and I am blue,
I will not say I'm in love.
Maybe I'm hurt by things I shouldn't be;
Maybe I help in ways unhelpful.
Maybe love can be complicated,
But that doesn't change standards of expectation;
It doesn't change how I feel.

If we're purple, call us luxe romance or call us passion,
But do not call it "love." I will not rename it; perhaps
It is only a dream, sigh, "almost," but I cannot settle.
We should try harder, go on an extensive search,
Even possibly admit it doesn't exist outside
Of what I believe and know. But in that case,
It would need to be held close and careful,
Alone if necessary, before I ever deny this color
I have seen with my heart.

PLEASE FORGET

Forget me...

Because "up" to you is wealth and prestige...

And "up" to me are the heavens and the shining joy of sunlight.

Because "down" to you is crude eyes casting their judgment.

To me, it's the child whose hope was taken.

(If you could be lifted, I would do it, but...)

"Right" to you isn't about reclamation or redemption, only vengeance.

Because "left" is what you think of when you see me,

Instead of how I can stay faithful to what I value

(While able to impart compromise and reason).

Because we're going in different directions,

And it's too painful and confusing...

Forget me.

THE STORYTELLER

Reading you was vain; your eyes held a pool of lies
As easily as they could hold back gallons of pain,
And wink of love all the same.

I turned your actions over in my head
Day by day, but the story always changed.
Once having taken every letter you'd spoken as

Permanent ink passion in dismantling your words,
I broke the spine, which kept this fiction world
From being written away.

HOW CAN WE SAY GOODBYE TO LOVE?

How can we say goodbye to love? Where has it gone?
Does not the God we know speak of forgiveness?
And if it were not an error small, but great in
declarations,
Will we look at preference more than substance?

Do we prefer mere commonality and
Not in upholding love we share it?
No one understands all of our ways...
There is no perfect love if we abandon love's chance.

When did our hearts choose to suffer lesser things,
Choose odds to necessity? Was it ever authentic?
If you no longer hold the faith and void its holy call,
Love has not fled but has been rejected.

Why would any bid it farewell? How can it come again?
Unless... and I hope, your mind is changed.
Only then, you'll see, our bond
Could have made it.

LONG-DISTANCE RELATIONSHIP

We fell into a portal,
Grey to prismatic skies—
A ticket to a new place;
Heads stuck in the clouds.
In the gatehouse,
In the waiting area,
I thought of you;
How you said you'd
Meet me halfway.
It sent my heart into flight;
I need you to cross over,
But now your plane is canceled,
And I'm mid-air and crashing.
Don't worry, I'll be fine
Having crashed and
Flown before we met,
I know how to survive.

FISHERMAN

Was I wrong to feed?
We all share an appetite...
Did I cast the hook?
I cast true looks of desire,
Not artificial bait and lie!
You preyed upon me,
Fisherman! But in a rush,
You could not wait and
Take the necessary time.
The colors of your line,
The lure, poetic almost...
Glittering, spluttering,
Jerking back, exposing you.
I got away, and you were mad
That day. Imagine me,
Close to death, and
Leaving hungry too.

ROSE-COLORED MEN

Rose-colored glasses are lifted, but I still see red—
My Savior's blood wasted on lust that fled; passionate,
Warm blessed love, exchanged for the blush and ache of
Shame.

4

CREATIVE CULTURE

ATTRACTION

1

Miss's smile is like freshly fallen snow.
Her arms are the wind, and the
Wings of butterflies her hands.
Her skin is full of nectar,
Legs: silk,
The posture of a gazelle.
Her voice is the early canary.
And she dresses in a summer garden.

2

Mister's hands are like lily pads
Surfacing a thick pond. The movement
Of his arms familiar rock slides,
Legs: lighting, chest of a tiger.
He has gemstone skin and words
From a rolling river. His smile is light
Peeking through an Ecuador,
And he dresses in magma.

WHAT IS WISDOM

Who has seen the children so devout? Notice the glimmer in their eyes being held, for each their lifetime, I know well. Ha! The youth, eager for school!? As public teaching should be—a grand unraveling of mysteries. Bright wonders explored. Depths of life made fearless by divine love—all of them have unique perspectives and abilities. I know that if their passions continue under the stern teaching of the Lord, after hours, they'll flourish, aspire, and found a wonderful oasis. And they'll enjoy every moment of their work endeavors; and the aid, and company, and diversity of one another. Glory!

They've been learning about the senses this past week, how to hone them with everlasting delight. For God has given sweetness in all things. Now they can savor the smell of freshly juiced pineapples and run out to inhale the freshly cut lawn before they frolic in its prickly pleasure with great peace and gratitude knowing Him. Mostly His ways, His heart, how to not deteriorate the delights of His gentle gifts by abuse or misuse. They won't ignore their mother's warning about asking permission before skipping outside in the morn. As they know, she too is a present, from Him, of presence. From where they first drank, thirsting to be nurtured. Dependant and granted. She knows about the early morning dew upon the grass and that her beloveds' little feet need to wait until a later time before their little immune systems are exposed by their open toes in the waving field. They trust guidance now. Grace! Its heart has been restored.

They also hear lessons about overseas people and places, and how pineapple trees and their exports do not exist in every location. They then taste from their cups with a special appreciation. Bless it! They won't be soured by sickness or complaint. Greater interest and greater gladness will be known to each of them, and in seeing this look of radiance in each other's faces, they will be faithful and successful in all things. Yes, they will embellish every moment, for they are being taught great wisdom!

True education, a loving venture.

SPEAKING YOUR LANGUAGE

Teach me to speak your language
So we can talk of love.
I will learn to understand you and
Be a resonating voice.
I wanna cross barriers that divide us
Like lies or accents on our tongue.
I will be more fluent in listening and
Try new styles of speaking
So we can talk of love.

BLACK BUSINESS

Diversity and black owners meet down
the blacktop street—
Where black businesses are springing up on sight.
Music is playing, and people are out,
The sidewalks are merry, full of bustling crowds,
Merchants to the left, merchants to the right.

Smiling shoppers welcomed inside.
All walks of life engaging in
Black business.

It's the conversation!
Why it's the pinnacle of the song!
"One day, I will not be a slave,
But I will have my own;
Hands working for my favor;

For pleasure work and freedom."
Labor to a better life,
The type men, women, and children hope to have.

It's the conversation

Heard on news and radio stations;
Flyers uptown, and
Word of mouth—it's gotten out, now
Roaming the world!

Local designers,
Sustainable fashions,
Urban garb for the culture.

Black natural hair and
Skincare shop selections.
Black cosmetologist salons,
Black dermatologist appointments,
Black therapist offices just over a block.

Black nurses and scientists in nearby
Hospitals and labs finding cures
And treating genetic conditions.

These know the heart of the city.
These know the condition by witness.
These know how to handle the proceeds
And puts 'em back in local communities.
Black entrepreneurs and black leaders

Making investments for their children's

Education and future positions.
They see how it's all connected

And give guidance across the world—
Black-owned plants overseas—their reflection
In and throughout all humanity;
In boys' and girls' eyes, young and old.
They want to see healing and build growth

Through seed and stem, root by root and
          reach by reach. Keeps history from repeating
Itself, assures no one for color gets maltreated.
Knowing God's light is love, not a pigment of skin.

Ask the black preachers of mixed congregations
Raising, feeding, holding, and tucking our neighbors;
Reading and studying life's ways and adventure!
Black teachers, back to basics. Black united.
Back to beauty. Black artists sure to highlight

The blacktop streets, galleries, and museums,
The modern and memorial. Black ambition
Praying and paving forward.

TEACHING LEADERS

On two occasions, I saw a leader on his knees.
The first time, he knelt to a child's height
And faced him, curiosity to curiosity.
He took and brushed the boy's shoulders,
Regarding and commending how much he'd grown.
Both their cheeks raised twice the other
For a while then—the student of his learning
A sort of greatness had in getting older.

The second time, I oversaw him praying
That the kids would not be led astray;
But age well, a God-honoring life,
Overcoming trouble, and causing none.
As a fellow teacher looking on, I recognized
There's so much to our being, are evermore stages
And folders deep in our core. More inside people
Than meets the eye.

CARAVAN WITCH SHOP

I took a step into an unknown place, into a caravan, vivid in color; a nearby traveler's. A few stairs up led into a sparkling shop, where a lady rose from behind a center counter, and after peeking over, stands, greeting me first.

I give a generous "Hello," followed by a question of whether or not she was the keeper.

She chinned, "Why, yes. I am the pink potion, puff smoke, hot liquid antidote, owner of this showroom. The colored powder, house pill, flower grinder, Devil's prayer. Oh, and I could be your fortune teller, crystal ball, tarot reader.

Pan the ceiling," she continued, "My own painter's hands charted these stars to tell guest like you I know the signs. I can line skies and palms, trace out your destiny. You don't have to believe coming in; you'll have seen some things by the time you leave. I help the hurting get their closure from their loved ones who're passed on. I can tell you if your future's worth living; can make a spell to turn it around.

I'm a seer and witch who does good. But, if you'd rather brew and serve the teacup than join my party, look around. I have sage, spirit quartz, and books establishing the route."

"Oh, no," I hiccup, "I'm too afraid of God. I was stopped by the sight of your ruby red car and the floral mural, but I'm at peace with God's plans. I trust His wisdom too much to change my own path. He's like a father, He's been a friend, and I'm too in love to question Him, too in love to compete with Him.

It was then she said, "Compete," and asked me to elaborate.

"Well...excuse me," I say. "In the nicest way, I believe you're playing God."

"God gave me my abilities. I simply play up his supernatural side."

"You said you use a devil's prayer. Who's permitted to ally with His enemies?"

"That is a figure of speech," she groans and sighs, "said for how often I have been misunderstood."

"Understood," I nod, remembering old mistakes, explain, "You should never call yourself the negatives others might see. I could think you're an artist, I should say you look lovely, but only God knows you in and out. But I am only in and out. Thank you for sharing the space. I did not find any new bracelets. I sought unique pieces, found a unique person. I saw your jewelry while you were outside, that's what brought me by... thought there could be more. Nevertheless, I'm glad for you opening your door."

NO CRITICS

Forget judgment.
Forget the peering eyes over your shoulder.
Forget the compliments and critiques,
The jealousy or mockery.
Forget everything.
Resort back and intake the power of "The Creator."
Start from scratch,
And make what you want to see.

ART

It is the object to your surprise;
The framed thing that makes you
Think beyond the box—
A statement and conversation;
A single artist and entire communities.

"We are creations created and creators;
Visual art made by an artist's imagination—
A drop of dedication and fun intelligence
Shaping the world's experience,
Vibrantly or in desaturation, but a certain nudge
For the heartbeats' desire or satisfaction."

What joy!
A tool in a hand of passion,
The emotions elaborated
To concrete from abstraction.
What a time!
Of mindful endeavors solidified
And shared back to a soul.

HISTORICAL FICTION

Suppose we expand the earth into a book of fantasy,
Within logic, still, shouldn't it sprout its wings to live
and breathe?
In the most unique ways, I see the glories of purity.
Every page of life it vanquishes
Each drop of will in mankind's abilities.
But a reckless writer pours immoral blood inside
the pen,
Delves into darkness, but exposes no consequence.
Thus reason parallels into the real world's soon end.
So take caution, dear writers, to lead your spirit well,
Before we follow your imaginations.

FINDING INSPIRATION

Wait for inspiration—
Wait with a sip of coffee.
Wait by reading a morning devotional.
Wait through prayer.
Wait while preparing breakfast.
Wait as you join someone on an errand.
Wait as you go on a stroll, and intake nature.
Wait as you knock out all work on schedule.
Wait as you lay to check friends' socials
and local events.

Wait for it to speed out of your fingertips,
Ideas returning zealous to burst out again.
Be sparked amidst unwasted opportunities.
Inspiration is nearby, so wait and never give up
searching.

AS NEW AND AS OLD AS FOREVER

Lady of music gleaming like the early hour, fresh sunlight through the window, new love put to paper.

At the piano, she writes and plays rainfall upon keys.

A spring song, a slow dance; she listens and pens it in cursive—

Patiently, ambitiously. A heart-cry.
Forever good-morning.
Her love.
Her love.
Her old love, an epithalamia score.

He enters like a wave delivering the rising sun, washing the room in adoration—bleeding sunlight's glow and spotlight.

New love, her love wakes as new and as old as forever sun.

A golden tear into the sea and across a golden line, her heart sings for a particular ear. Her cherished journal cradles each word between champagne rose covers—some in bloom, others slow buds. Inside is a thin script, a noted page, drenched in liquid heart.

Inside their marriage is an ever-garden.

THOUGHT

Let it free,
Chase it down,
Lose it again.
Watch it glint at you and peak,
Watch it wane and flood,
Watch it spiral and explode—
Some are bad,
Some are good,
Some seem forbidden.
Seek it out,
Teach it,
Or keep it guessing.
Welcome its silly side,
Welcome its opinions,
Gather it together
For clear thinking.

BIRTH PAINS

Work can either wear you out and kill you or make you feel alive. Depends on why you labor, for what in which you strive. Laboring without birth is detrimental. You must have sight of giving way to something, especially sentimental, or it's vain at completion.

She's going to be so precious to me when she's finished (everything I'm writing and creating). I have been identifying as a poet lately and artist as well. And I can't wait to have my artwork and books printed in my hand. I'm so excited to see someone else delight in my efforts, like a proud mom. I love what I do. I know it is important. I want to reach souls. People matter. Big and tiny, you see?

Giving birth to anything sweet is such a blessing. I thank God for these moments. I'm constantly growing and having to work harder, but it's worth it. When it gets plain old tedious and rough, I hate it. But the result will wash troubles away. Those times are incomparable to how we gain. I'm optimistic today because of the thought alone.

Are you thankful for what you do? It counts. You impact things around you. Keep your work life-giving; don't let it be deathly to you or others. Look forward to something. Labor hard, and watch yourself push through. We're in an age of opportunity and information to even help you envision, know, and answer to what I am curious, what will you be having; a boy or a girl?

RHYTHM OF LIFE

Profound persuasion, music...
Keying hearts
Stringing it for better or worse,
Playing into life bad rhythms,
Beating a conscious,
Echoing curses,
Or
Sweet melodies,
Orchestrations of beauty.
As symphonies compose harmony,
Tuning positivity.
Sound waves spring songs
Hum and carried throughout the day.

HERE'S TO...

Here's hoping we all want
The same love deep down.
And that somehow my words
Can resonate with everybody.

SEAMSTRESS

Plumb
Violet,
Ripe
Red,
Light
Dusk
For a summer
Morning,

Mix, cut, mend.

Cross cotton dye,
One shoulder in,
Fasten pattern
To swim
Diagonally.

Textiles
On the
Tabletop
Toss and spin
In stripe,
Plaid, and
Geometric
Squares.

Four by four fabrics
Trim and thread
In wool, linen,
And silk scraps
By the dozen
Spread.

Add ruffles
Mesh white,
Knit embroidery
On sleeves,
And whisks
Of sheer material
Lying next for
The seamstress

Like dew
Clinging
Over lime
Under peach
And faded
Blue skies.

INK INTERLACING

I left my daughter choice stories of fantasy.
She is a free-spirit who rarely sits for study.
But I saw her life shape out as though she knew
What to believe and not to do. So I think
Her readings exceeded fiction and were
Interlaced with the greatest of lessons.

5

DEAR ONES

HOME

Turn any doorknob
Under any rooftop,
Wherever I am met
By warm embrace
And conversation,
Wherever a caretaker
Of my body and soul,
That is the place
I call home.

LOVE PUT OUT MY EYE

Love put out my eye;
So much I hate to witness.
How do you watch your closest suffer
Because encouragement fails them?

Love put out my tongue.
I grew numb and speechless,
As no attempts of mine
Could spare you every harm.

Love put off my hands,
Sorry I stopped reaching out,
But I became so broken I then entrusted God
To hold and heal in ways I cannot manage.

RELATIONAL FAITH

You had parents twice to pray for, none violent but too "good" a kind; blind to real love for focus on upholding reputations and standards higher than God's. Like gaining wealth to serve for pride and vulnerability taught as weakness, a disruption to the image. Their deceptive successes neglected what you needed most.

My family understood my deviance and musical direction; said it was a gift from God, but none of life is easy, and I should remember His purposes; and that they would support me however they could. I received preparation and a blessing. I learned how to take care of people deeply. Moved into my new place, thought of how I could give, and met you at my Sunday service. You were reserved, but I learned your story after sharing a lot of my own.

We both grew more to understand the difference between faith and religion. You entered intercession for your family shortly after your rededication to God. We're roommates now, and I watch you study for your degree. You love God, and life, and music like me. You told me you never felt so liberated and grounded at the same time, and that you have newly found satisfaction and hope in life.

LOVE KNIT QUILT

I am the quilt across my grandmother's lap, equal lovely to her as she is to me.

She is warm steadfast affection. She is safety holding wisdom.

I am knit, stitched—eyes to heart, heart to eyes—in her guidance.

I look at life in her care. Taught to get away in private,

wear glasses like she does if it helps me see more clearly, and study—

and not for the sake of education, she says, but the beauty thereof.

Grandmamma is perspective; I am the colors of her youth. She implores adventure,

able to recite multitudes of stories. Her smile appears different

from pictures she shows me, it's worn and older; still, it's shown

As boldly as her speaking of old tears. She explains certain times

will have suffering, more than what she fears for me, "But collections of teaching

like scraps of fabric when put together presents a bigger picture"—

To remember that the world belongs to someone close. To reflect on what is said of the cocoa maker, the shea butter planter, the sweet tea lover,

and the sun rising brown sugar giver, who gave her all she has. To know most,

who holds me, made with affection, and can keep us together despite odds.

Grandmother's lap is a cushion I love to return to.

I am a quilt adored.

NEVER OUTGROW MY LOVE

A child develops by hugs, kisses, nicknames,
And when they're softened to see all of what
Life has in store to give and embrace.
When they grow inside your heart,
They grow into their heart,
Eager to eventually fill their own
Hungry little eyed child.

Promise to allow my love for you forever, always.

I will never outgrow that smile as it changes
Tooth by tooth. I will find new pleasure
In your laughter, how it heightens and settles,
Rediscovering your amusements in our times
Spent together hysterical over typical weirdness,
And growing more and more fond and thankful
For our relationship.

Promise to allow my love for you forever, always.

HONEYBEE

Did you know love is something
We do or don't progress in?
I remember how it felt being
Listened to and ignored. Excused
Because the busy bee had already
Zipped sealed their attention.

I can't say that won't happen sometimes
But I will assure it doesn't silence you forever.
Despite being tired, despite other issues,
I have learned to clear the cloud
And reprioritize as a way to care.

So in instants appearing inconvenient to the eye,
Try me, it may not be inconvenient to my heart.
You are honey through the noise.
Share everything trite and grand.
I want to know, and want you to know
You are soul, you have a voice, and it is heard.

THE SPLENDOR OF SWORDS

You taught them to honor good fighters—
Good, meaning who they are before the win.
To care about integrity over anything obtained.

Your wife wants to honor you,
The soldier of her household—
The arrowed heart pouring out
For her and your' children.
Authentic love is prize,
Not flattery or praise;

Sacrificial men and women,
Implementers not imposters.
Charm is laughable
If you've been served by a protector.
Trophies rust, love refines.
Darling, you are the splendor of the sword.

PRIVACY

Trust is a doorway, an entrance into my life.
Its sheer curtains on the frame form a barrier
Between your inner world and my space,
Which can be pulled aside for peeking,
Or you can wait for the moment the wind blows
Welcoming all to know how I am and have grown
Recently. I love sharing, but I value privacy.
People who force themselves on you experience
You differently. Their days around are not the same
As those who naturally get closer because the timing
Is right.

B.F.F.

This isn't a child's dream, is it—
        to want an endless friendship...?
In former days we'd be joined at the hip,
        playing long hours,
Laughing solely at the strange,
        adorable ways of one another.
It is a blessing to have grown and matured.
        Work is essential,
And meetings must be planned,
        but haven't we aged into greater awareness
Of what it means to be together?
        Even in distance,
My friend's face is close-knit behind mine.
        You say I say the funniest things,
Yet our humor is the same.
        We joke at love
And find our embarrassments hilarious—
        An oath to never take
The shallow things of life too seriously.
        I've adopted your pains,
And you share my sorrows; though hated occasions,
        it's laid the foundation on why
We'll honor kindness. Sure, the world
        has hurtful moments,
But won't we be timeless friends?

WHAT I HAVE IN A FRIEND

Because I have a friend,
I have a treasure box of memories—
A holder of my secrets;
A holder of my favorite things,
And shared trinkets.
A chest that spills my interest,
A chest of golden goods.
The special find in life's journey.
The reminder of why I explore.

SOME PROOF

Catch my smile each sunrise.
Is it as bright as you are to me?

I want you to see the beauty of forever,
And I think I could prove it

If you saw the way your happiness
Set me alight every day.

PEARLY GATES

Friend, you have pulled me through many trials,
But you cannot pull me through the pearly gates.
You'd vouch for my innocence, name no one more
moral,
But if you knew who you could save instead,
Your passion would burn away. This is not our home
Or place to invade—the vanity, the fierce tenacity,
May be just one letter in the reason for no invite.

Alas, my friend,
If a pure standard is set,
I must bear the toll alone.
Face full right of obligation,
And I am found unrepentant of
All the care I failed to give...
Now, I understand....

Tell the forgotten beggar before you beg or plead for
me
"Call on rains origins and do not call on me
That the world I left behind may drink."
Tell, tell the suicidal mind, people drowning and
thirsting,
I blasphemed God, the Savior.
I did not know how He could be the key.
Do not lead them astray.

LOST MEMORIES

Memories steal the moments of our lives and sometimes gives them back. Sometimes, it keeps them in a small treasury to be opened only in the eternal realm, under God's eye. There it knows charity and would rewind, sit, and pull you close to remember sweet forgotten graces. But when it visits our world, like many of us, it often forgets all morals and taunts instead, making us plead for a recollection of the good times and better days.

6

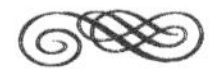

SEASONS

HUMMINGBIRD CAKE

Hummingbird cake.
We resound "Happy Birthday!"
You gleam a smile endearing in the candle-light.
What a gift to watch you grow;
You admit a penetrating glow,
A private prayer, and the following blow.
May God always be with you through love
To bless you,
Hopefully in some ways through me.
You dip into the icing and lick your finger at the party,
Terrible quirk, but it's yours and for those close.
I'm simply glad to have a part of your life.
There is no present here, like you.

SOVEREIGN SILENCE

Soft cotton eyes that could fall at the slightest wind,
Your yawn stretches, crinkling your kitten nose.
Lucent beauty—gone sound asleep
In the cradle of the moon,
Gone away
Under cover of the night,
Do not wake. I will no longer speak.
Do not paw your eyes; they are saying hush.
Rest, and let them shut. Sleep in the sovereign silence.

SPRING IS IN TOWN

Leap about!
Run around!
Spring is in town!

Precious petals,
Warming winds—
Love swept up in everything—

Fresh linen and ideas
To soak in sun;
Mini-vacations for family fun!

S-P-R-I-N-G!
The day feels yellow, ya know?
But your lips and cheeks
Plus your swim floaties
Add a dash of reddish-pink,
A splash in the seasons glow!

Opening are the windows!
Opening are the flowers!
Opening are the sheds for things

    we'll play with for hours!

Bikes, and rackets,
Balls, and baskets,
Chalk, and water guns!

S-P-R-I-N-G'S IN TOWN!
Thank God!
He always brings her.

COOKIE BATTER

Scraping the bowl of the last mix.
Mixed it up well, it's a great batch!
Roll 'em out good, shape 'em,
And lay 'em on the oven mat.

Cousin, the cookies are almost ready!—

A little more icing, a lot more sprinkles.
Adding the love and special touches.
Dress the gingers and hearts in sweet powder.
The cookies are almost ready!

JUICE/ COLORED SWEETNESS

Purple kites
Blue skies
Green grass
Yellow sun
Orange flowers
Red fingers.

Sweet children
Calling for
Colored sweetness!

Fruit juices
Popsicles
Butterflies
Running sprinklers;
Them all splashing round and round
Shimmering rainbows on the ground!

AGELESS JOYS

7, 37

Son and father

Returning a Frisbee through the air.

17

Teenage

Car gliding, windows down, catching the breeze.

37, 7

Mom and daughter

Cheering for the little league sports team.

27, 27

A young couple

Deciding to travel as their new hobby together.

7, 17

Two sisters

Playing patty cake with one another.

17, 17

Two brothers

Making a handshake with each other.

7, 7

Classmates

Dressing up as pirates and goblins.

27, 37

Married

Getting ready for a formal affair.

7s

Neighbors

Rolling down hills laughing and stumbling.

47

Independent

Climbing mountains. Marking ventures.

17s

Teenagers

A game of hide-and-seek in the dark.

27s

Best friends

Who knows they can detail and converse about anything.

SUMMER LOVE IS THE LIFE WE LEAD

Summer luxury vehicle burning over a cliff. Drunken friendship poison exploding.

Revert to the cave, to winter. Stowaway. Hibernate. Milkshake a new life

before the seasons change from the time of bondage to freedom.

I want to be free when summer comes. Days before summer are labor.

The foreshadowing months for affording desire. The work for play.

Your working, your mental efforts, your spiritual journey are exposed

In the light of summer. Then is ice cube water under the sun or a far

too hot disappointment—a lingering, traveling nagger Persons who cherish nothing,

Or summer fling is slingshot promise. "God bless. Aim for the skies." Hit gatherings

Of chilled lemonade glass passing to active, sugar fill your passion children,

And husbands sweet, and wives perfect, and friends. Friends who're acting out

Nostalgia or silent figures in a game we group play around beach water

Into the night, lit by a sparkling flame. People ready to throw past tragedies

In the bonfire; the world ready to look out for one another and spin in a

Year-round summer's joy. We are the future. Forever young! Leaving behind

Standards, broken, and rewriting or digging up to resurface only what

Has always mattered. The stress, the devil's pitchfork, is dead. The pain

Made insanity. Our history has paved the way, the endless road of

Summer freedom—redemption from all mistakes. We are the generation,

The teenagers, the kids, the adults of victory. We have The scars of yesterday

And daydreams of sand bruises. Nothing wasted. Lavish. We hone every wave,

Riding the open-top convertible ever grateful. We will cry tears caught by

The sun's very own kisses of "underappreciated miracle." Summer love is

The life we lead. It's our heart beating music for us to forever toss our head,

Jump, twist, rock, and sway to. I want summer love, a look into the clearest

Sunset, knowing this is the way of the entire mended world. Summertime love.

Love ripened like the fruit this time of year, a storm turning juice and hidden waterfall—

The tiring hike's relieving river dive. Once spring itself is washed and stowed away,

Summer awaits to be the life of peace—the sleep between hammocks and

Toucan forest and edge of the boat harbor waving adventures—a motion of

Never-ending bliss.

THREE SKIRTED GIRLS

Three skirted girls
Twirl around fresh fallen leaves.
A show of fabric
Drifts in the wind—

Mahogany, amber, and tangerine breeze.
Three skirted girls
Gallop and fall into musical laughter,
Their melodies echoing between the tree branches—

A dance of thanksgiving,
Compliments in cheer.
Three skirted girls
Hurry into the field!

"The Harvest Banquet is at 5 up the hill."
It smells of spice and gives a thrill!
"Glad you're each here,
Three skirted girls."

AUTUMN LEAVES

Leaves whiff to and fro.
Their reds, their yellows
Painting my heart with colors of warmth
On the chilliest day.
Drifting down and thoughts of the sound
Remind me of kids crunching them underfoot on
playgrounds,
A reminder of youth, and perfect love stories.
This present luxury is the coziest
Unwinding, breathing
Aromas of cinnamon sticks
And stained pages of good old books.
Oh, the papers and stories I began,
For what cannot be read will be written!—
Under orange ceiling, with black ink,
With my beloved cat as black as night.
Ah, I'm not superstitious...
She passes me by,
As consistently as the time.
My! It's gotten late.
Oh, praise God for this season before it's too late.
Rise from the kitchen, turn off the light,
Close the curtains, dress for sleep,
And fall into bed like an autumn leaf.

SOLE WHISPER

The sky is quiet

Despite the occasional thunder,

Quiet not silent—

Dull... blue,

Speaking through puffs

Of static, hushing.

Raining.

Relaxing.

I am out to visit the book store,

Feet trickling drop by drop, pattering down

The puddled sidewalks to the awning edge.

I exhale and fasten my umbrella,

Shaking off a bit of the water.

Someone walking out is

Holding open the entrance,

I nod at them and go in.

Once the door shuts,

It is quieter,

Quiet not silent—

Dull… black carpet,

Low-volume indie

On the speakers.

Perfect.

Classic.

I know what I'm here for; still, I roam around a bit.

I made sure my pockets are only the amount in dollars

and change I'll need.

I am only looking—turning each isle skirting my eyes

top to bottom of the columns,
Gliding my hands over a few spines—Margret.
One of the books is facing forward; poetry.
I don't see any other copies and wonder if it's by a local
Artist. The store owner's cat approaches and purrs at the
end of the walkway as though she wants to give me
The information, or maybe she's my reminder to not get
carried away—maybe all my inner dialogue.

Me, her, and Margret passing messages
Through a glance. Others are also browsing
And mostly keeping pretty quiet—
Quiet, not silent.
Dull... some of these book covers—
Souls whispering from the shelves.
Old.
Pine.

"I want you, Margret. I know you'd love to be with me."

"I will never die!" she assures, "You can always return to
me."

I walk over to check out after picking up my original
desire, and I say across the counter,

"I love this place."

"Yea, it is better in here than out there today. Traffic's slow,

But the environment's always great. I can actually count

On getting some reading done."

She has light coffee and preoccupation on her breathe.

Multiple ideas on mind it sounds;

Multitasking, a quiet sense of business—

Quiet, not silent.

Dull... eyes and work shift.

Unknown adventures call out

Of a thousand hearts:

Books.

People.

SNOW ANGELS

Snow angels are a lovely joy to make—
Laying white gown, spreading white wing,
Flying in the cloud of snow.
A wonder! How many wonders drift over our heads?
May I chase them down for eternity
Beside the God who could replay and pause time
So I can see His glory, like the snowflake—
What delicate craftsmanship.
The passion one must have to care over each detail,
The heart to keep it soft,
The humility that it can go unnoted,
The pride that He alone has to marvel.
I am more than snow angels made.
God is more than living.

WINTER DEPRESSION

Cold-hearted winters—
Log sticks cold.
Blue log without fire.
Body limbs blue;
Blue veins with
Cruel attraction—
People forced to shiver,
To want, and reflect on
What is not where desired.
Bedside silence.
Mid-hall occurrence.
Midthought silence.
Winter teaches survival.
You find the means to
Keep yourself warm,
Gather match and wood,
Or freeze over.
But once a fire is going,
Oh, once the glow is sparkling
Spice riches of life...
We love the air we breathe.

THE JOY OF WINTER

God's got us bundled up,
Wrapped away from cold.
Yes, zipped and buttoned up,
Wrapped in chunky scarves and coats.

We rub our hands together and gather heat in them
With breaths. Soon inside-out are reddening bright
After amused friends tease the fight for warmth
Hit snowballs to our back;

This is the fun of winter.

Icicles on near lamppost gleam.
Snowfall is down every neighboring street.
And brisk flurries in the night sky meet
The quiet morning a bit softer;

This is the beauty of winter.

Open boxes of candy-cane, cups of hot chocolate
topped in whipped cream,
And a gingerbread house to taste and decorate

In gumdrop roofing—from our nook of laughter,
prayer, and great thankfulness
For chance to sing favorite blessed Christmas carols;

This is the sweetness of winter!

WINTER WARMTH

You're coffee amidst the snow, my dear—
The warmest kiss after the bite of ice.
Your smiling eyes melt the hardened heart and
Call hidden love to life. As your voice pours out
Laughter and you place your hand in mine,
You're mittens in the snow—my dearest
Hold through winter sights.

CHRISTMAS ADVENT

Christmas anticipation!

Are all dressed for the occasion?
I think our ornament of St. Nicholas,
Who's stuck in Santa's suit, would agree
He is not ready.

Later, our kids and their friends share worship and
Give a jolly act; my daughter plays Mary, her friend
Elizabeth.
My son tells me he's happy knowing Jesus came.
My Mary cries and dances and cries and wipes her face.

My love and I pray after,
Asking for holiness;
We know so many graces and
This light we shall not quench.

Oh, cherished advent!—

Gift wrapping for local neighbors, and people
Preparing breakfast for all unfed! My family
Also converses about our favorite gifts of life
While reading through the Gospels;

A great blessing is the gift of Christ!

Let us venture out into God's grace
Singing carols, skating lakes, celebrating
The good news on every avenue!

TOMORROWS'S PICK AND PLAY

Tomorrow is the secret mix of trinkets
Behind someone's back;
The closed hands presented in front of you,
A choice always uncertain.
How much this game is safer known
It's held by a good friend!
So no matter what happens, you enter trusting
You gain through every pick and prospect.

7

SELF-GROWTH

I WANNA WAKE WITH LOVE ON MY HEART!

I wanna wake with love on my heart!—
If you ask how I desire the day to start—
A thousand times, I will declare differently;
No single picture. Delight's without limit!
And though I'm a dreamer, it doesn't have to
    be perfect.
I'll take my child's toes in my face,
Or being in the arms of my significant other,
Or my ordinary independence—the full
    kick and stretch
Of free responsibility. On my couch, in a tent,
As an overnight visiting friend, or paying rent—
After a contemplative night and grateful rest,
I will wake at my best with love on my heart!

TWO GREAT DIFFERENTIATIONS

I find myself torn between two great differentiations—
Wanting forever or nothingness. Declaring,
    PERFECTION! I pray it never ends!
    Or groaning, "Why is there pain?
    Why did life ever begin?"
I welcome life when it's a glimpse of glory.
    I cherish good experience
    And love thoughts
    Of paradises.
Please, don't allow these to fade away but come again;
    All people are pleading for eternal bliss.
    There must be more than worries and stresses..
    Than disappointment.
Than seeing selfishness heighten, then
    Wither and injure.
    These almost make us forget
    Well days of blessing,
And welcome death when life's a glimpse of hell.

INDEPENDENCE

Alone is: strolling down an avenue,
Head high in your own tune,
Grabbing frappes at local brews,
And planning things to try and achieve.

It's an easy peasy day;
Some would disagree, but it is my sanctuary—
At peace with self, at peace with God.
My downtime in great company.

I push myself not to be alone,
To go and spread the love inside me
With other walks of life,
To join the great surroundings.

SELF-CARE

Submersed in a raspberry tub,
Slight foam, gentle lather, and soak;
Rose petals fragrant and harp aria afloat.
Ahhhh... a grace evening of TLC
For the body of a warm spirit.

BECOMING AN ADULT

The "mom's and dad's" shoe will fit one day.
Their neat hair, accessories, and blazer suit
Will take perfect shape on you but in your
Own style, smile, and prime example of adulthood.

Quicker than you know. So surprisingly quick,
The younger you will awe at making it through times
You thought would last forever and couldn't be
Overcome, and if for no other reason than that,
be proud.

It's the start of being an adult—owning your decision
To keep growing and looking forward. You'll need
To set a direction that keeps you brimming in hope.
Don't think too much; you know your wants.

Aim for them; go for it, accepting no discouragement.
Not because you're setting out as an activist
Who's ready to trail blaze, fist raised in passion,
Daring to counter culture for the sake of a needed
lost message

(Though you just beautifully may). But because therein
Resides a small cry for empathy and self-love, which
Should not be disregarded for any of humanity. Because
You want to encourage other's genuine fulfillment, and

you, yourself, can and should be pursuing it.

Know what and who you love and why.
This is how mature adults conduct themselves,
Able to live their lives day in and day out;
They stand with backbone, with something to protect.

And be civil. People who think freedom is a wild thing
Rather than a part of a loving construct forget
We inhabit a world not our own, made by a Creator
Who's instilled natural laws that put away the foolish
who cause and reap harm.

Don't stunt your growth in this path, but have
Understanding, thriving in wisdom and virtue; honor
God's image. Bear kindly with people and allow
Others to help you. Sometimes things will get hard
but pray, never impossible.

PIÑATA BABY

Piñata baby,

No kicking or crying;

Life is a celebration

Despite a killjoy.

Harness emotions

By friends, hobbies,

And journals.

Confetti outburst.

No holding hurt.

Free shown colors;

We'll watch you release 'em.

Full control, full expression.

Take hits and mold 'em,

Profit beauty from pain.

Life can be a celebration,

Firework baby.

13:10 JOHN'S OLD SKIN

Whatever was done to stain your clothes
Stripped you naked
To rid and change,

But you carry the ink in your shoes' soles,
And everywhere is grey
As it bleeds through.

Unknowing of the error made
You work double-time
Covering the mistake,

And you're exhausted day by day
Because you've yet to slow down
And wash your feet.

MISERY ISLAND

Do not visit Misery Island,
The journey is unbearable.
The stress of sharks alone
Will devour you whole.
So do not set to sea,
Spare yourself the storm.
Make the best of hope,
Where now life is beautiful.

RAINBOW RAIN

I should pack an umbrella.
I cannot predict the weather,
But I can be ready for what is
Likely to come.

My family received news that
A newborn is on the way,
And my godmother is making
Preparations for the Baby Shower.

Everything can't be anticipated,
But a forecast helps with expectations.
Heard your parents got a new job
So you may have to switch schools.

Know life happens; have it covered.
Prayer takes us into the Ark to brace
Each storm. Give God your worries,
And He'll present how to plan ahead.

Rain is a possibility. But I've outlasted
It enough to recall promise so near it doesn't
Have to let up before the clearest span
Of colors are caught dripping around me.

WILDFLOWER

In a little pot of dry soil,

A hand was first to sprout;

Startling but lovely,

As though a tiny flower.

Next, a knee broke out,

Then a foot, a leg, an arm.

Lovely but startling...

Its every root overgrown.

BUTTERFLY, BUTTERFLY

You are made to break a chrysalis,

But no one ever tells of

How the caterpillar turns goo;

They feed, gain strength,

Then enter isolation,

A stage of disintegration

(What sort of insanity!?),

But they transform.

Scales are their new form.

Leave the green.

You are made to do it.

Our reappearance showing

Being fragile is okay,

And one of the most perfect

Little beauties in life.

How special you will be for

Innocent eyes. Remember love.

Remember life before the gob.

Shoulders back to use your wings,

For flying in the blue sadness,

Adding color where it wasn't before.

DANCE FOREVER!

So many mirrors have watched me dance!
And so many floors have felt the trance
Of glee and rhythm, turning in bliss!
I feel quite weird in some instants, but
I'll dance forever! It is a gift!
To experience the outflow of happiness!
Love watches me, no mind to looks,
Go sway with ease. Move and step!
Motion together! Wild and free!
Dance forever!

NATURAL HABITAT

I'm an ever-growing plant in my skin with my hair.
Reminiscent of the trees. Bold upon the world.
Chestnut girl. Standing tall. Tender branches.
Fluid and natural. Free! Raw!

So happy with myself. So woman. So beloved.

The after shower rain fresh upon your skin, isn't it like dew on the grass? Even indoors, we're alive as the wild. More. Wipe the mirror, look through the steam, and think of the outdoor air. You're you, a part of it all. No matter looks, aging, or repute, you're here; God seeing the naked you. Rinse. Feel washed from the daily disappointment. God fills your day with a new breath. Breathe in this love until you drip it, known, no matter how soaked your steps. Run your fingers through your hair and regain who you are.

CREATE LOVE

Create love
No matter how hard to do so,
For it is something
That truly lasts forever.

And if the devil bickers,
"Love holds no satisfaction,"
Create it anyway for your soul,
Wherein God redeems its value in salvation.

So many things are fallen,
So much including love.
Build it up again,
Build it on God to hold firm!

8

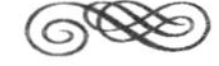

COVENANTS

PRAYER NEEDS

Dress me like the lilies,
Feed me like the sparrow,
Take care of me, dear God.

Show your face to me,
Grace and sanctify,
Soften my heart, oh Lord.

And bring rain for
Poor and harvest,
Please, Thy kingdom come.

Answer our earnest prayers,
In the name of Jesus,
Amen.

LIFE THOUGHT OF ME

Life thought of me...

Not after providing

My total pleasures and dreams,

But when giving me life,

And I marvel on why?

This world bruises imagination,

Limiting it for nothing more

Than to hurt me, but Life—

Remarkable, glorious Life—

Says to me it is beyond this world

And is galaxy and Spirit,

Purity and eternity, and

I am created for far more.

Now I can't help but think of it.

THE FOUNDATION OF HOME

My home will have a law.
It will have Christ, and what it looks like
To abide in Him.
It will have holiness and obedience from
Purpose to encouragement.
It will have freedom, joy, and prayer.
It will have guidance and sweet relationship
Between us and God the Father.
It will have forgiveness and never giving up
On each other.
It will have love and learning to love,
And tough love from explanations and reasoning.
It will have grace. It will have sacrifice and peace.
It will be an oasis because it is firm.
It will have trust in God's faithful words.
It will have humility and modesty.
It will have close intimacy
And pride in family.

IF I HAD A PARAKEET

If I had a parakeet,
He'd sing a song of the Lord's grace—
Of how He comes as a sudden wind,
Shortly missed and wished again.
Of how His love is the present air,
Enlivening and fundamental.
Of how I wonder of each breath,
The brisk breeze and surrounding gust
(Far beyond felt but seen!)
Of how His Spirit lingers close,
My favorite part, this leads the song;
And he would tell the mockingbird,
Who nosy came but savvy went
Carrying these words throughout the world
So it could know to praise and worship.

LOVE SURPRISES ME

Love surprises me like an angel on a window seal suddenly sent from God. I accept it saying thank you, not to be received as paid due, rather, favor goes out freely

From His embedded nature. Yet I know the Lord should have this, to Him it does belong; He is selfless, and I am taught—to give to love its rights, out of a full

Heart of desire—allowing inspiration's visit and flight. Still, what a shock the more it comes with ease, but I think it should remain odd, if happiness is a light

Pouring past the blinds, uncontrolled and voluntarily; doesn't that amount? A grace I cannot earn given through a life I did not bring about. How do angels fall

When basking near His brightness? You explain some find more adoration for the night... Oh, because I have witnessed how much can leave, love surprises me

In how it chooses to be here and known, a part of my forever.

A SEASON FOR REASONING

The One who changes
Winter to spring,
Spring to summer,
Then summer to autumn's fall

Can surely change the season of death to life.

The One who changes
Babe to adolescence,
Adolescence to adulthood,
Then adulthood to elder's grave

Will surely change our winter to spring.

A LIGHT MESSAGE

I catch a subtle hint
That all will be okay;

It's a silent message sent
From habitual honesty.

GOOD AND EVIL SEEK MY HEART

The Heavens seek my heart,
So send me there.
Hell chants my name,
But it's not as tempting.

Should I gain the world
To both our destruction?
Where is love among
The dying?

It sounds from above,
Pleading an exchange—
Corruption for everlasting grace!
It lives beckoning my faith!

BELOVED INNOCENCE

Beloved innocence,
Held like the grape for taste—
Held delicate, lest you are crushed
And lose your flavor.
Beloved maturity—
Delicacy savored—
Led like a stream to poverty
By an adoring Father.

KING CREATIVE

King Creative recreated famine grounds,

Taking its broken boys and girls

Into His hands like crumbled vessels

For molding and reforming. He ordained

The sons' princes and daughters' princesses

And moved them onto His solid foundation.

Then He gave them calling to illustrate

His glories and to remodel the fallen kingdom

Using His imperishable materials.

RIGHT HAND OF THE THRONE

Imagine looking up to scale a sitting giant.
His feet firmly put, shoulders resting, and
The rest of Him is light—no chest or belly,
No face; just legs of fire and arms extending
From bright amber rays.
He reaches for me, taking my whole body into
His hand like a mustard seed, and I feel grounded,
Visible, and fruitful at the single touch.
The Creator enthroned. The seat appears between
The radiance at certain angles and His Son
At His right hand, who finally by a sole glance
His pleasure is my sun and crown.

SOUND OF LOVE

Love is the sound of heaven.
God is the sound of love.
God gives life to hope.
Hope gives life to love.

A FLOWERS, A RED

I have a rebel heart. It eases out at night,
Sending for my father, out from His garden,
Teasing Him to say, "Please, don't play with trouble."
But I'm unsure if He calls this time.
I am lost among another's, and I hear foreign voices.
And notice many a flowers, a red, and many
A red, rich, drops of blood.
I've never known a thorn nor been strangled by a vine.
I've wandered too far off and faintly remember home,
Only that it never bore a pinch or a scar feeling of
Hopelessness.

GENTLE COVERING

Lay down and meditate on the
Blanket of grace, the simple
Love holding the world, and
You with gentle favor.

HIS WORD BROUGHT THE MORNING

The word brought the morning—
Brought the morning light,
Brought the cicadas song,
Brought my Spirit alive—
And I sing, and I'll worship
From Genesis to Revelation
Because my God is here,
And has been, and will be.
And He speaks life to my soul
Through His word of love!

BONDSERVANT

Will you honestly not surrender to anything but your pride? Not I. No, I would gladly lay down my life and become a slave of love. Indeed few things are worthy of being served, but this is quite the labor for ambition! Humbled low to honor this Highness well, a master I cannot surpass. Have it lifted high! It does not reign without merit. It leads selfless, returning more than what I owe. Love gratifies me. My Lord is love, and I will give my Lord everything.

9

VOWS

AGELESS LOVE

Ageless love,
We will live in
Eternal arms.

FOLLOWING LOVE

Follow God, my dearest, and I will follow you.
I've been independent so long I'm head-strong,
But if you keep God the head, His will be done.
Let us be led by the One who does no wrong.
I know I'll have to kill my natural reflexes
That think because you're imperfect, I'm wisest.
God knows our weaknesses and supplies
    for every position.
So, I will not seek my way of foundation,
But trust you because I trust Him.
And if you abuse His sacred way of submission,
I'll pray that you come to your senses.
Love is why we enter our pursuit.

LIPS OF LIFE

Let me speak all the words that could melt your heart;
Show you deep affection until we're not apart.
I want no pride or hesitation. I insist, no fear.
May love for you conquer and state each feeling clear.

Keep all your words that wound, no need to fight;
Do not bottle up your anger, but change your mind.
See gently, think again, and let us reason.
Why would we hurt the ones there to listen?

In every word of kindness, I await...
For hearing the voice of glory woos me awake.
It runs a soul far into pretty places.
Talk no vain curses, but bless us with your language.

I ADORE YOU AND ONLY YOU

I adore you and only you
With lightest ease and deepest affections.
Our connection made in heaven;
Darling, a grace given present,
Know forever, you will understand that.
I adore you and only you.

I adore you—
Your quirks.
Your wit.
Your heart.
Your Spirit.
You're charming, and only you can charm me.

HAND HOLDING

Holding hands is a simple notion
Stating pride in your significant other,
Glad to identify with all of who they are.
The connection claims their affections as your own
And to protect in the warmth of your palm.
It's for those humble and unashamed to show
They've fallen into grips of another soul.
Holding hands is a simple notion
For you and me.

CARRY MY LOVE

Here's a little something—
I bought it with my heart;
A present to go with you,
A way to carry my love.

SEND A LETTER

Most writers have read modern poets

Idealizing old-fashioned romance:

Wine dances, park dates,

Phone calls, and invitations.

And I bet a part of them is waiting

At their mailbox after events of memorable conversation,

Hoping by a small chance someone might send a letter—

Something special to say that of the connection.

Handwritten, fragrance scented, and lick-sealed.

To make one half-faint, full thrill,

As distant love arrives from vintage daydreams.

A PARENT'S CARRYINGS AND DELIVERIES

What could I buy for you?

Would we ever shop together?

I'm carried away by the wind—

Coast to coast, scene to scene—

In car rides out with you

For groceries or whatever else,

Like walking down the baby aisle.

Oh, the little things I imagine!

I coddle my arms,

Pretending to be a mom

And watch for what you think of it.

And when you say I'd be perfect,

I nervously toy over

My engagement ring.

I think I have the heart, but already fear

Whether I'll have a mother's strength.

Perhaps it all comes on the day of delivery...

Like you bringing over take out when I'm hungry.

Love is pretty good at stepping up and inquiring

Specific needs, and picking up details between the lines—

'Cause on the phone, I said, "Oh, I'm fine."

Yea, God is faithful.

My love's been faithful

To assure we talk each day.

God's known me longer,

Watched me closer,

Has seen me through every way.

He's the perfect Father to exemplify.

I feel His heart in us,

So odds are our children will also.

To be in great hands!

God carries me!

I should not be too uneasy.

Judging now and I feel uncertain,

But on that day, I know I'll be different.

I'll be a parent doing all it takes

To look after them—restricting certain things,

And, in numerous ways, leading and encouraging!

I'll hang on to their growings in confidence,

And keep hold of their hand when they fall.

Likewise, in time, maybe not how I want,

But for my needs, God will provide!

COMMIT TO ME

Commit to me.
Commit to eyeing me with
Protective instinct and admiration.
Commit your heart, your body, your friendship.
Let us find rest in these places in one another.
I almost worry about not being enough;
That time will create a lack of interest and distance
Between two people who were once so fascinated
By the other's mere existence.
But if you're for commitment, for me
Being who you will always be committed to love...
I know we'll last forever.

HONEY

Honey,
Your lips must be made of honey.
You're so organic,
Mix in romance,
And it'll never lose flavor;
A simple kiss I'll always savor,
My delicious
Honey.

Recipe reserved—

Tasted on my tongue;
Sweet honey made with love.
No one else can drink a drop
Of my seasoned passion
Without stop of
Full devouring—
Honey.

MANY MASTERS

Yes! Why would a lady have the mind to submit to the husband she loves?

Or why should a vigorous man need the God above? Who has time for it?

We're already committed to the government and the boss's demands at work.

Once arriving home, there will be no more sacrifices, even if it's a connection

For the better good, understood. Debt is our bondage and all the prices of education.

Too many things call us to submission.

LIP STAINED

Leave me traces of your love,
A kiss saying you'll always be here—
The kind that lingers while you're gone,
Your lip stain to await your return.

BED OF ROSES

Love spreads like sheets
Over a warm bed of roses
And calls forth the laughter of a child.
Beloved, know love goes with you
Beyond your first footsteps and our last.
Once loss covers the land in winter,
Love spreads as sheets of snow,
And when it—perfect—melts away,
Love goes out and picks a rose.
Reborn through a bed of roses!
Give not your rose to our grave,
But to life another, for love lives on.

WON'T WE DANCE

That young night at a glance
Built our romance—
Sparkled sky, sparkled eyes...
Like this moment full of promise...
But it's so much deeper than the surface.

Won't we dance?

Red dress, tux with vest;
Dolled up cliché, out to make a memory.
A surprise we're together after all these years?
The love in us transcends the stumbles and the
Missteps.

Won't we dance, again?

Smiling pride—mister and wife.
A joy being this close inside, alive in time,
Counting the rhythm of songs we can't forget...
Only to keep it intimate... as the days we first met
And agreed to have fun with the gift of music,

Won't we?

SISTERS OF THE BRIDE

These are the sisters of the bride:
She and she—the gate,
She and she—the guard.
Their arms around her
Are like the Lord's—
True love, love eternal.

A heart can be carried off in vain,
Charmed in deception, but
Where is virtue; what is pure?
Her sisters sought protection,
Reaffirming the will of God.

They have held me accountable,
Ensuring I walk toward love,
Ensuring our affections
Are lasting, are firm—knowing two
Are brought together to form a bond
That should not be broken.

GARDEN WEDDING, LOVE CEREMONY

Love—
A God forgotten,
A word distorted,
A man's and woman's.

Love—
A burning passion,
An admiration,
The satisfaction.

Love—
His veiled lady,
Her trusted partner,
Beauty, and romance.

Love—
Ever-growing,
Outspreading,
Unhinging.

Love—
A fleeting pleasure,
A fleeting pressure,
A fleeting promise.

Love,
Do you take me?
Do you take me?
To be your lawfully wedded.

It would be a garden wedding; the guest list—skeptics—beneath trees ornamented over rows of chairs dressed in burgundy covers, and laced, and tied in flowers. The evening a floral canopy seated with excitable elegance. The pianist leads their entrance—the best man, the maid of honor, the flower girl, and the crowd in stance.

Then the groom awaits
The bride in white,
And her bouquet:

Brown and light roses,
Blush white ranunculus,
And orange tulips,

But
Down
The
Aisle,

She
Couldn't
Go.

Love—
A God at center,
A word of substance,
A crown of thorns.

Love—
A burning passion,
An admiration,
The satisfaction.

Love—
His bride and joy,
Her devoted partner,
Favor, and worship.

Love—
Ever-growing,
Outspreading,
Reproductive.

Love—
A forward progress,
A forward pride,
A forward praise.

Love,
I do.
I do.
'Til death do us part.

The wedding is in the garden this afternoon. The list of guest are optimistic, and the scenery exquisite—the trees are a floral canopy blooming and graced in drapery, overarching cream covered seating lined in well-dressed, excitable friends and family. The pianist leads their entrance—the best man, the maid of honor, the flower girl, and the crowd in stance.

Then the groom awaits
The bride in white,
And her bouquet—

Ivory roses,
Yellow peonies, poppies,
And jasmine vines,

And
Up
The
Aisle

She
Will
Go.

I CANNOT IMAGINE

I cannot imagine

A heartfelt orchestration

Of our midnight kisses of love,

Which proves not only

That we are charming

But woven of royal blood,

With a spirit from the heavens

Passionate to fight

And lead a life into an affectionate kingdom.

I cannot imagine you've been set to roam the firmament

In a faithful life of your own—

Serving your heart to glory,

Building up an army,

Only soon to be refocused by the Lord.

Saying, "Yes, further My grace and patience;

Marry your desire!"

I cannot imagine love refining

To greater measures than already found.

I think what tragic use of time wondering...

Yet am maybe sensing it's not in vain—

And truly written.

That we will hand in hand, chest to chest,

Weep over battles but rejoice in this:

Our sanctuary, promises, and covenant;

Our togetherness in all its bliss—

Making paradise to come most evident.

I cannot imagine.

I cannot.

THANK YOU

Before you close this book, I would like to thank you for reading! I poured as much of myself as I could inside it! If along the way, you shared some of the emotions I felt while writing, then you have already imagined with me, celebrated with me, exhaled, and experienced the way of thankfulness I want for you to know I have, in the thought of you, right now!

I grew during the creation of this collection, and I know I will continue to grow for every new heart inspired in it. I have been a wanderer. I have found my footings and passion! I am glad for you finding my book in your life! Where to next—through mysteries, through falters? Through the light of Love's venture! From here on, everywhere, in grace!

Sincerest blessings, and thanks!

ABOUT THE AUTHOR

Heart of Glory Publishing presents Bohemian Bride, a book of prose and poetry by author Janae Ballard. Born in Birmingham, Alabama, Janae continues to create works infused with a spirit of youthfulness, divine groundings, and pure contemporary looks at life and love.

Visit www.ballardjanae.com for more of her writings, resources, details on her artistry, and information about future releases.

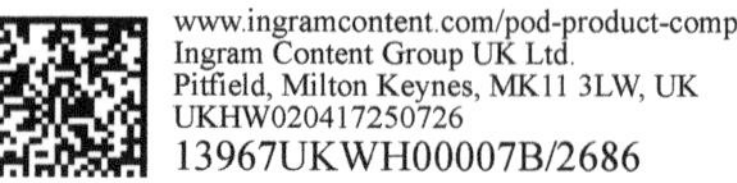
www.ingramcontent.com/pod-product-compliance
Ingram Content Group UK Ltd.
Pitfield, Milton Keynes, MK11 3LW, UK
UKHW020417250726
13967UKWH00007B/2686